PERTH AUSTRALIA

D1147607

Steve Parish Publishing Pty Ltd

Perth's central business district, looking northeast.

PERTH

A jewel of a city, Perth's glittering crystal towers stand proudly side by side with fine sandstone buildings erected by convict labour. Set on the sweeping, scenic curves of the Swan River, the capital of Western Australia enjoys one of the world's great climates, with warm, dry summers and crisp, cool winters which promote outdoor living.

In Perth, you may laze on the silver beaches and in the sapphire waters of the Indian Ocean, picnic on the banks of the Swan or sail its sailboat-studded expanse, enjoy cultural events such as the Festival of Perth, visit fine galleries and museums and sample wonderful food in some of Australia's finest restaurants.

I find Perth endlessly fascinating. When I visit, I wander the historic port city Fremantle, spend sunny days at unspoiled Rottnest Island, and always end up in the wildflower garden that is Kings Park, gazing at the combination of riverside parks and lakes, city centre and broad Perth Water that make up one of the world's great cityscapes.

• Capital of the West •

Western Australia occupies
one-third of the continent of
Australia. Perth, its capital, has
a population of over 1 200 000.
Set between the Indian Ocean
and the Darling Ranges, this
sparkling city stands on a
broad sweep of the Swan River.
The Narrows Bridge (left) spans
one end of Perth Water.

◆ Riverside elegance ◆

A view across the Narrows Bridge shows the elegant integration of Perth's central business district with King's Park (left), Perth Water (right) and a fine system of riverside parks, gardens and lakes. In the foreground, just over the approach to the bridge, can be seen the historic Old Mill, a beautifully restored relic of the early days of Perth, built in 1835.

◆ Perth's history ◆

Perth was founded in 1829 as the Swan River Settlement. In 1850, convicts were brought in. They erected many of the city's finest buildings before transportation stopped in the late 1860s. In the 1890s, the discovery of inland goldfields brought a building boom.

• Old and new •

The second half of the
twentieth century brought new
discoveries of minerals in the
northwest of the State and
Perth underwent another surge
of building. The best of the
city's older architecture was
complemented by stunning
modern developments, and
some notable restorations,
such as that of Bank West
(right), took place.

This fine building once housed the Perth Court of Petty Sessions.

Built between 1852 and 1854, this was the original Perth Boy's School.

A stained glass window in the very modern Forrest Chase Shopping Centre.

The sumptuous blue facade of the Central Park Building.

• Hay Street Mall •

Hay Street was once a narrow, busy thoroughfare.
Today, it is a broad mall, bordered by stores,
boutiques and restaurants, sprinkled with
outdoor cafes where connoisseurs of coffee
can sit and watch the world go by.

• London Court •

London Court, a charming olde-worlde avenue of speciality shops built in half-timbered Tudor style, runs from Hay Street Mall to St George's Terrace. Its above-entrance clocks feature jousting knights and St George and the dragon, and Dick Whittington stands guard inside. This popular landmark was built in 1937.

Left and above: Murray Street Mall

◆ A place for picnics ◆

The grassy banks of the Swan River provide a
perfect venue for family activities, especially at
weekends. Barbecue areas and shady picnic
spots are scattered along the river's winding
course from Perth to Fremantle.

◆ Fun on the river ◆

The Swan River, with its broad stretches of safe water, provides a playground for locals and visitors alike. Sailboats and powerboats are everywhere, and waterskiing and parasailing are popular. For the less adventurous, there are ferry cruises to points of interest such as the vineyards of the Upper Swan and down the river to Fremantle.

On the wings of the wind, Swan River.

Jetskier, Swan River. Over: Catamarans on Perth Water.

Marinas offer safe moorings for the prized craft of Perth's sailboat enthusiasts.

• City of the black swan •

Western Australia's faunal symbol,
the black swan, sails proudly on its
flag (above). At left, a family party
of black swans take refuge beneath
the soaring sculpture which graces
the grounds of the Burswood Hotel
and Casino.

◆ The black swan ◆

Perth's swans are privileged citizens, supervising the activities of their human friends (left) or rearing their families of fluffy cygnets in the quiet backwaters and meanders of the river which bears their name (above).

Over: City lights, seen from Kings Park.

• From Kings Park •

Kings Park offers a great view of Perth's city centre. The platform shown at left is part of a larger area where many of Perth's people gather on public occasions, such as services held at the park's War Memorials (right).

• Enjoying Kings Park •

Occupying land set aside in 1872, King's Park is an oasis overlooking the city. Covering 400 hectares, it contains superb Botanic Gardens, nature trails (top left), picnic places, a tower lookout and the famous Pioneer Women's Memorial Statue and Fountain. Fraser Avenue (lower left) is one of several public roads lined with stately trees. The park can also be enjoyed from a horse-drawn carriage (centre left).

⋆ Western wildflowers ⋆

Western Australia is world-famous for its
springtime wildflowers. Perth's gardens
feature these beauties, while Kings Park
offers a feast for the senses which ranges
from sumptuous everlasting daisies (left) to
stately kangaroo paws and banksias (above).

• A city near beaches •

Beaches of silver sand stretch north and south of Perth. The view of Scarborough Beach at left shows just how close the city centre is to the azure waters of the Indian Ocean.

• Cottesloe Beach •

Cottesloe, with its leisured
atmosphere, good waterfront
restaurants and famous golf
course, is one of Perth's most
popular family beaches.
Weekends see the surf
lifesavers set the flags to signal
safe swimming on this sun-
drenched strip of coast.

• Hillarys Beach •

Hillarys Boat Harbour and Beach at Sorrento, north of Perth, is a favourite place for water sports. It is a magnet for families living in Perth's northern suburbs, providing a great place to have fun.

• Fremantle •

Fremantle stands at the mouth of the Swan River, 19 km from Perth. Its population of 25 000 is multicultural and its restaurants outstanding. It is full of lovingly restored, convict-built offices and warehouses, many housing vigorous and talented exponents of the arts and crafts. Fremantle is a maritime city. The view at right looks over Success Harbour and the Fishing Boat Harbour to the working facilities of the Port of Fremantle.

◆ Historic Fremantle ◆

In May, 1829, Captain Charles Fremantle planted the British flag to claim the west coast of "New Holland". The twelve-sided Round House (left), was completed in 1831 and served as a gaol until 1848. It is Western Australia's oldest surviving public building. Fremantle's streets are showcases for gracious colonial buildings such as the ones depicted at right.

Over: Cafes at dusk, Fremantle.

• Rottnest Island magic •

Rottnest is an island 11 km long and 5 km wide,
lying about 19 km off Fremantle. It is a magic
place, where visitors forget mainland cares and
relax, sail, fish, holiday or explore the island
by bicycle (no motor vehicles are allowed).

• Sea friends •

Denham, on Shark Bay, is around 800 km north of Perth. At Monkey Mia, 26 km further on, wild bottlenose dolphins swim to the beach to visit humans (left). The interaction attracts pilgrims from all over the world, some arriving by charter aircraft from Perth.

Steve Parish has recorded Australia, its wildlife and its people with his camera for many years. Steve's aim is to show people the marvels that exist in this long-isolated continent, with its unique cities, landscapes, plants and animals. His passion for Australia, and his awareness that urgent human action is needed to preserve its wildlife and places of beauty lends intensity to his superb photographs and evocative writing. Steve and his wife and partner Jan founded Steve Parish Publishing Pty Ltd to share with the world their vision of Australia.

Steve Parish

PUBLISHING

© Copyright photography and text Steve Parish Publishing Pty Ltd 1997
First published in Australia by Steve Parish Publishing Pty Ltd
PO Box 2160 Fortitude Valley BC Queensland 4006 Australia

Photo page 62: Jiri Lochman

Text: Pat Slater

PRINTED IN AUSTRALIA

ISBN 1 875932 84 4